# I Can Make It Myself!

**Group** LOVELAND, COLORADO

## Group's R.E.A.L. Guarantee to you:

Every Group resource incorporates our R.E.A.L. approach to ministry—a unique philosophy that results in long-term retention and life transformation. It's ministry that's:

R E A L

**This is EARL. He's R.E.A.L. mixed-up. (Get it?)**

**Relational**
Because student-to-student interaction enhances learning and builds Christian friendships.

**Experiential**
Because what students experience sticks with them up to 9 times longer than what they simply hear or read.

**Applicable**
Because the aim of Christian education is to be both hearers and doers of the Word.

**Learner-based**
Because students learn more and retain it longer when the process is designed according to how they learn best.

# I CAN MAKE IT MYSELF!

Visit our Web site: **www.grouppublishing.com**

**CREDITS**
Contributing Authors: Jacqui Baker, Sarah Macy Bohrer, Julie Bowe, Sharon Carey, Robin Christy, Laurie Copley, Nancy Wendland Feehrer, Sheila Halasz, Beth Rowland, Deborah L. Saathoff
Editor: Linda Anderson
Creative Development Editor: Jody Brolsma
Chief Creative Officer: Joani Schultz
Copy Editor: Betty Taylor
**Cover**
Art Director: Jeff A. Storm
Designer: Alan Furst, Inc.
Photographer: Tim O'Hara
**Interior**
Designer & Art Director: Jean Bruns
Photographers: Paul McEntire, Tim O'Hara
Illustrators: Terri and Joe Chicko, Kate Flanagan, Rusty Fletcher, John Jones
Craft Construction: Katie C. Brakefield
Computer Graphic Artist: Shelly Dillon
Production Manager: Peggy Naylor

Library of Congress Cataloging-in-Publication Data
**I can make it myself: Bible story crafts for preschoolers.**
    p. cm.
  ISBN 0-7644-2225-1 (alk. paper)
   1. Bible crafts. 2. Christian education of preschool children. I. Group Publishing.

BS613 .I2 2000
268'.432--dc21
                                  00-035386

10 9 8 7 6 5 4 3        09 08 07 06 05 04 03 02

Printed in the United States of America.

# CONTENTS

# INTRODUCTION

2 Corinthians 3:17 tells us that "where the Spirit of the Lord is, there is freedom." In a classroom craft project, it's important to give children the freedom to express themselves. If we want all the crafts to turn out exactly the same, we might as well give children coloring pages and tell them which colors to use. This book will allow your children to "color outside the lines" as they complete crafts they can be proud to take home. For instance, if you look at the craft on page 58 titled, "Salt and Light," you'll see a colorfully painted salt project that illustrates the story from the Sermon on the Mount. The end result is pretty, but the process is what's exciting and meaningful for the children. As it touches the salt, one drop of paint explodes almost magically before their eyes. Another drop mixes with the previous colors to create new colors. No finished product is expected. Children feel no pressure to conform to the teacher's sample. The children may express themselves in a manner that pleases them. This is fun and exciting for children and makes learning more effective.

Peter Kline, in the book *The Everyday Genius,* says, "Emblazon these words in your mind: learning is more effective when it's fun." When a child can have pleasure in the process of creating a craft, the craft will have more lasting impact on the child. Crafts that concentrate on following directions and creating uniform results can help in refining listening skills, but they usually do not evoke the pure pleasure a child enjoys while creating on his or her own. Children need to be able to use their minds to create meaningful projects. This process doesn't always yield an expected product.

Many parents make the mistake of asking, "What is it?" when they look at a craft project. Sometimes the project isn't anything; it just is. Parents need to understand that some projects have no unified end result. Sometimes the process of the craft is much more important than the product.

If you want to help parents appreciate preschool art projects, try some of these ideas:

● Tell the parents about the day's theme so they can see how the project relates.

● Write a brief Scripture passage or title on the craft.

● Invite parents into the room, and let them see for themselves how involved children become when they enjoy freedom in the process.

As a teacher, you need to know what you can expect from preschoolers who tackle craft projects. As you plan your craft time, use the following guidelines:

Three- to five-year-olds have a very limited attention span for following directions.

They can listen for only two to three minutes without interaction.

Expect children to use glue in unconventional amounts. For this age, part of the pleasure of gluing is to see how much can ooze out of the bottle! Adjust drying times for this. Glue sticks make very appropriate alternatives for some projects.

Little ones have a very limited ability to create anything that looks like a person or an animal. They will rarely draw body parts in any uniform manner.

Scissors skills are very crude. Don't expect that they can cut on the lines. More realistically, expect them to enjoy snipping and the pure fun of seeing the scissors move in their hands.

Preschoolers usually have no qualms about mixing paints together. In fact, they are built to enjoy mixing colors.

Expect children to try techniques other than those presented. They are curious and imaginative; encourage rather than stifle these qualities in the classroom.

Expect some children to love tactile projects and some to be afraid to get their hands anywhere near a mess. Both extremes are normal. Adapt messy projects to help those who feel uncomfortable being messy.

Some children respond to projects better while listening to music. Try playing music in the background during craft time.

Kids are still developing eye-hand coordination. Expect children to get frustrated if you require too much detail from them.

Expect varied amounts of involvement. Some children will want to spend twenty minutes creating and recreating a project. Others will finish in a couple of minutes and need an alternative activity. Whenever possible allow for both extremes. Remember, the goals are pleasure and learning, not to fit learning into a designated time slot.

Use the wonderful craft ideas in this book to follow up your own presentation of the Bible story. The crafts will really help your children remember the stories you've taught them.

God created differences, so please take the time to appreciate the differences in children and accept differences in crafts. "Where the Spirit of the Lord is, there is freedom."

*Sheila Halasz*

Sheila Halasz has advanced degrees in early childhood education and elementary education. She has taught in public schools and has started a licensed Christian preschool in her church. For twelve years she has operated a home child care business that caters to preschoolers. She has co-authored nine Christian resource books for young children as well as children's curricula.

**BIBLE FOCUS:**
God made everything.

**BIBLE WORDS:**
"God created the heavens and the earth" (Genesis 1:1b).

**BIBLE STORY:**

# Creation

The earth, the heavens, and all that they contain are the work of God's hand. From the tallest trees to the tiniest insect, he made every living thing. As preschoolers discover the world around them, they can begin to learn of our mighty God who created it. Remind them that God made them, too, and that he loves them very much.

# CREATION NECKLACE

**MATERIALS:**
For each child, you will need the following:

- Sculpey or other dough
- Small cookie-cutter shapes
- Shoelace or yarn
- Rolling pin
- A straw
- Five or six beads (optional)

# How to make the "Creation Necklace"

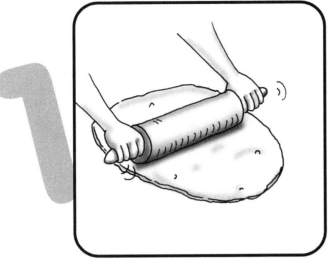

**1** Have children roll the dough to about one-quarter inch thick.

**2** Using cookie cutters, have children each cut out several creation shapes.

**3** Have children poke a hole in the top of each shape, and then allow the shapes to air or oven dry.

**4** When shapes have dried, have children each string their shapes onto a shoelace and tie the ends together. They can also put beads on the string if they are available.

When children wear their creation necklaces, they can remember that God created the heavens and the earth.

**ASK:**
- What did God make?
- How does God feel about all that he has created?
- Of all that God made, what do you like the best?

**BIBLE PASSAGE:**
*Genesis 1*

**BIBLE FOCUS:**
God is our awesome Creator.

**BIBLE WORDS:**
"God saw all that he had made, and it was very good" (Genesis 1:31a).

# Creation

**B**y merely uttering commands, God created the universe. God spoke the sun, moon, and stars into existence. With just the spoken word, all creatures appeared out of nothing. How truly awesome! Use simple shapes to show what God created in the beginning.

## SHAPES OF CREATION

**MATERIALS:**
For each child, you will need the following:

- Two-foot length of yarn
- Tape
- Green, yellow, light blue, and pink construction paper
- Star stickers and colored dot stickers
- Crayons or markers

# How to make "Shapes of Creation"

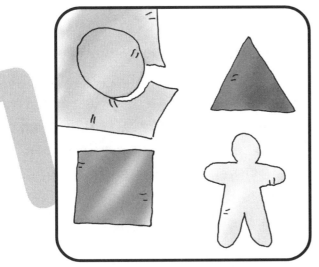

**Before children arrive, cut yellow circles, blue squares, green triangles, and pink people shapes.**

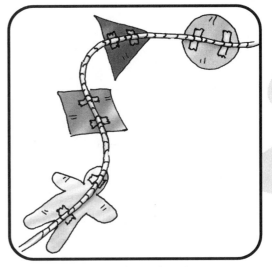

**Have each child tape the shapes onto the yarn in this order: circle, triangle, square, and person.**

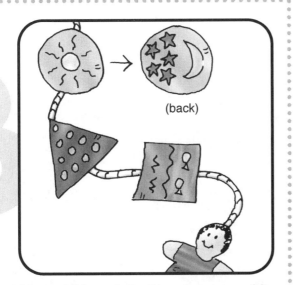

(back)

**Have children draw the sun on one side of the circle, draw the moon on the other side, and attach star stickers to the moon side. Have them stick colored dot stickers to the triangle tree.**

(back)

**On the square, have children draw a wave with simple fish and birds. On the other side have them draw animals. Have them draw themselves on the people shapes.**

After your children have completed their creation shapes, review God's awesome creativity in making the universe.

## ASK:

- How many different things do you think God made?
- What do you think about God who made so many different things?
- How can you show God how you feel about all he has created?

**BIBLE PASSAGE:**
*Genesis 9:8-17*

**BIBLE FOCUS:**
God keeps promises.

**BIBLE WORDS:**
"Whenever the rainbow appears in the clouds, I will see it and remember the everlasting covenant between God and all living creatures" (Genesis 9:16a).

## BIBLE STORY:
# The Great Flood

**B**ecause the people on earth had become so wicked, God sent a flood to destroy them. But Noah was a righteous man, so God instructed Noah to build a big boat called an ark. God kept Noah safe from the huge flood of water. After the water had dried and Noah was able to come out of the ark, God put a rainbow in the sky as a sign of his promise to never flood the earth again. Use this craft to help your little ones understand that God has promised to never flood the earth again.

# A SPREADING RAINBOW

**MATERIALS:**
For each child, you will need the following:

- Circular coffee filter
- Markers in a wide variety of colors
- Tape
- Spray bottle filled with water

# How to make "A Spreading Rainbow"

**1** Have each child lay a coffee filter out flat.

**2** Allow each child to choose four markers from a wide variety of colors. Tape the four markers together side by side.

**3** With the four markers you have taped together, have children draw a rainbow in the center of the coffee filter.

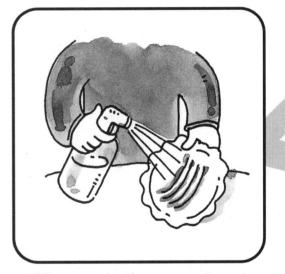

**4** With a spray bottle, spray water onto the rainbow on the coffee filter. The colors will run together to form a pretty rainbow.

After your children have completed their rainbows, talk about how God sent the rainbow in the sky. Allow them to repeat God's promise to us.

**ASK:**

● How do you think Noah felt when God made the rainbow?

● How does it make you feel to know that God has promised never again to flood the entire earth?

● We know that God keeps his promises to us. What are some promises you make?

**BIBLE PASSAGE:**
*Genesis 9:8-17*

**BIBLE FOCUS:**
God keeps promises.

**BIBLE WORDS:**
"The Lord is faithful to all his promises" (Psalm145:13b).

**BIBLE STORY:**

# The Great Flood

**A**fter Noah's ark landed, God promised the people and animals never to destroy the earth with a flood again. As a sign of this promise, God set a rainbow in the sky. With your kids, make this glittering rainbow to remind them that God keeps his promises.

## GOD'S GLITTERING PROMISE

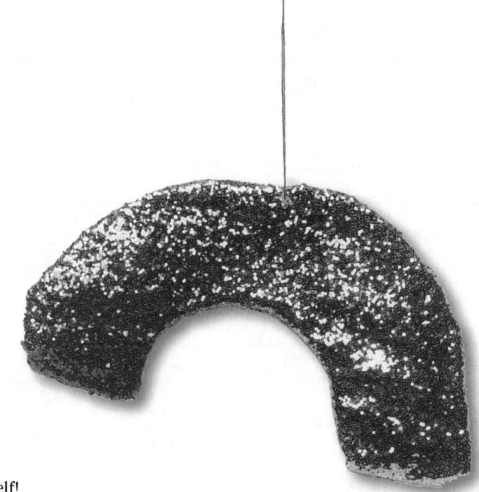

**MATERIALS:**
For each child, you will need the following:

- Wax paper
- Masking tape
- Glue
- Glitter, a variety of colors, in shaker containers

# How to make "God's Glittering Promise"

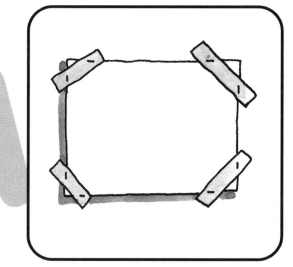

Before children arrive, tape pieces of wax paper to the table.

Have children thickly squeeze glue into a rainbow shape on the wax paper.

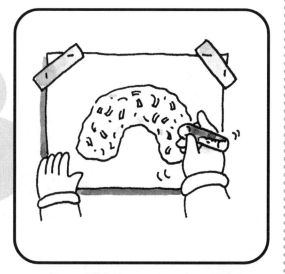

Allow children to choose several colors of glitter and then sprinkle the glitter onto the glue. Let rainbows dry for at least two days.

At home, each child can carefully peel the rainbow from the wax paper, and an adult can pierce the rainbow with a needle and tie a thread through the top. Hang the rainbow in a window!

After you've made your glittering rainbows,
**ASK:**
● Have you ever made a promise? What did you promise to do?

● How do you feel when someone keeps his or her promise to you?
● What is it like to know that God always keeps his promises?

## BIBLE PASSAGE:
*Exodus 8–9:20; 14:1-30*

## BIBLE FOCUS:
God keeps his promises.

## BIBLE WORDS:
"I am the Lord...I will be your God" (Exodus 6:6b,7b).

## BIBLE STORY:
# Moses and the Exodus

**G**od promised to give his people a land of their own where they could worship and be happy. Moses was to lead the Israelites out of Egypt and into the Promised Land, but the ruler of Egypt stubbornly refused to let God's people go. Finally, after God showed his power through a series of ten terrible plagues, proud Pharaoh freed Israel. Use this craft time to remind children of the power of God.

# BUGS AND FROGS

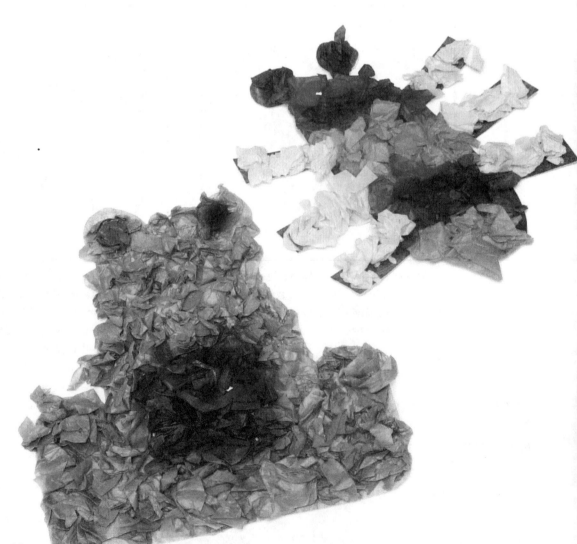

## MATERIALS:
For each child, you will need the following:

- Shapes of bugs and frogs cut from poster board
- Glue
- Watercolor paints, crayons, or markers
- Several colors of tissue paper, cut into one-inch-square pieces
- Refrigerator magnet strips

# How to make "Bugs and Frogs"

**Before children arrive, cut the shapes of frogs and bugs from a piece of poster board.**

**Have children each paint or color their frog and bug.**

**Have children wad up small pieces of colored tissue paper and glue them onto their frogs and bugs.**

**Have children add a magnetic strip to the backs of their crafts and place them where they can see them.**

When children have completed their frogs and bugs, they can use them as reminders of the mighty ways God showed his power in Egypt.

**ASK:**
- How does God show his power to us?
- How did God show his power to Pharaoh?
- Tell about a powerful thing God has done for you or your family.

**BIBLE PASSAGE:**

*Exodus 8–9:20; 14:1-30*

**BIBLE FOCUS:**

God helped the Israelites escape.

**BIBLE WORDS:**

"Do not be afraid. Stand firm and you will see the deliverance the Lord will bring you today" (Exodus 14:13b).

## BIBLE STORY:

# Moses and the Exodus

**C**hildren are fascinated with the account of the Israelites crossing the Red Sea on dry ground. It's a wonderful story about God's power, protection, and love for his people. God can do anything! Use this craft to help preschoolers learn the story of the Israelites escaping from Egypt.

# CROSSING THE RED SEA

**MATERIALS:**

For each child, you will need the following:

- One small tortilla
- A clean paintbrush
- Sweetened condensed milk tinted blue with food coloring
- One pretzel log
- Peanut butter in a squeeze bottle (If you are concerned about nut allergies, substitute squeezable cream cheese or frosting.)
- Gummy bears

# How to make "Crossing the Red Sea"

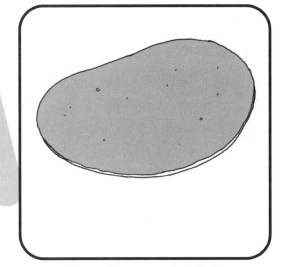

Have children paint their tortillas blue with the sweetened condensed milk mixture.

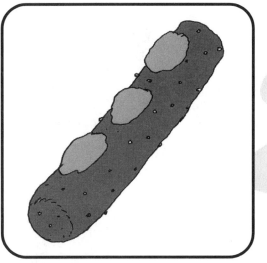

Help children squeeze several drops of peanut butter along the top of a pretzel log.

Have children stand their gummy bears on the pretzel log, using the peanut butter as glue.

Have children hold the tortilla as shown and then march the Israelites through the middle of the tortilla.

Tell the story of the escape from Egypt. Have children use their crafts to act out the Israelites crossing the Red Sea on dry land. Then have children push the pretzel log through the tortilla one more time. This time, they'll pretend the gummy bears are Egyptians. Have children roll the tortilla around the pretzel log to show how the Red Sea crashed in around the Egyptians. Then have the children enjoy their snacks.

## ASK:
- How did God show his power at the edge of the Red Sea?
- What did the Israelites do on the other side of the Red Sea?
- How has God shown his power in your life?
- What can you do to praise God for his power?

**BIBLE PASSAGE:**
*Joshua 6:1-20*

**BIBLE FOCUS:**
God helps me.

**BIBLE WORDS:**
"Be strong and courageous...for the Lord your God will be with you" (Joshua 1:9b).

# The Battle of Jericho

The city of Jericho, fortified with thick stone walls, could be conquered by only the strong hand of God. In obedience to God's command, Israel marched around Jericho seven times. At the trumpets' sound, the Israelites shouted. God brought down the city walls and gave Israel their first victory in the Promised Land. This upright puzzle can help your children learn how God helps us.

## JERICHO PUZZLE

**MATERIALS:**
- Coping saw (For teacher to use before class.)

For each child, you will need the following:
- A 12x6x1-inch piece of Styrofoam
- Brown and gray tempera paints
- Paintbrush

# How to make the "Jericho Puzzle"

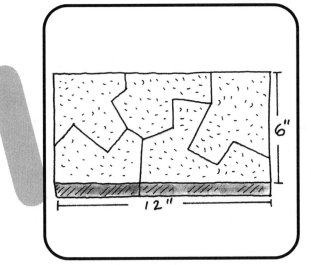

Before children arrive, find a handy person in your church to cut each Styrofoam board into five jigsaw pieces.

Have children paint each of the puzzle pieces to look like a wall of stone.

When the puzzle has dried, have children fit the pieces together to build a part of the Jericho wall.

Have children put their partial walls together to provide a place to act out the story of the fall of the walls of Jericho.

With God's help, Israel was able to conquer Jericho. As the children build their Jericho Puzzle, have them tell the story of how God brought down the walls of the city. When they've completed the puzzle, have them gently push it over and watch the pieces separate as they fall.

## ASK:
- Who brought down the walls of Jericho?
- How do you think the Israelites felt when God brought down the walls?
- How does God help you?

*The Battle of Jericho*  **19**

**BIBLE FOCUS:**
God is always with us.

**BIBLE WORDS:**
"And surely I will be with you always, to the very end of the age" (Matthew 28:20b).

## BIBLE STORY:
# The Battle of Jericho

The ark of the covenant symbolized God's presence among the Israelites. God met with Moses at the ark. The ark symbolized God's law and his holiness. Joshua prayed before it, just as Moses before him had sought God's will. The ark accompanied the Israelites across the Jordan River into Jericho and around the walls of Jericho at its conquest. Use this craft to help your preschoolers make a model of the ark and to remember that God is always with us.

# THE ARK OF THE COVENANT

**MATERIALS:**
For each child, you will need the following:

● School box with a hinged lid (or shoe box)
● White school glue
● Two ping-pong balls or Styrofoam balls
● Two small Styrofoam drinking cups
● Two sets of large paper angel wings
● Gold spray paint

# How to make "The Ark of the Covenant"

To make the angels' heads, have children glue a Styrofoam ball onto the top of each Styrofoam cup.

Have children glue a set of wings to the back of each Styrofoam cup. Bend the wings so the tips face forward.

Have children glue the angels to the top of the box lid.

An adult will need to spray the box and angels gold.

When all items have dried, carry the ark of the covenant as the Israelites did when marching around Jericho.

**ASK:**
- What did the ark of the covenant make Joshua and the Israelites remember?
- What helps us to remember that God is always with us?

**BIBLE PASSAGE:**

*Judges 6:36-40; 7:16-21*

**BIBLE FOCUS:**

God answers prayer.

**BIBLE WORDS:**

"The Lord will hear when I call to him" (Psalm 4:3b).

**BIBLE STORY:**

# Gideon

**B**efore an important battle, Gideon asked for a sign from God indicating whether victory was sure. Gideon set out a wool fleece and asked that in the morning the fleece be found wet with dew and the ground around it dry. The next night he asked that the ground be covered with dew and the fleece dry. God answered and gave Gideon the courage to stand strong in his faith. This craft can be a reminder for your children that God answers prayer.

# GIDEON'S FLEECE

**MATERIALS:**

For each child, you will need the following:

● White fleecy washcloth

● Blue T-shirt paint

● Paper to protect work area

# How to make "Gideon's Fleece"

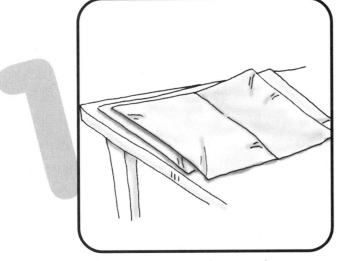

Prepare a work area where
children can paint.

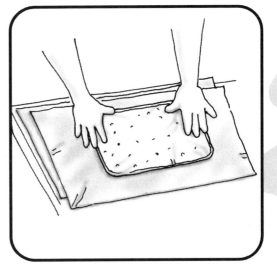

Have children place their washcloths on
a flat, covered surface.

Now have children add small drops of
paint to one side of the washcloth.

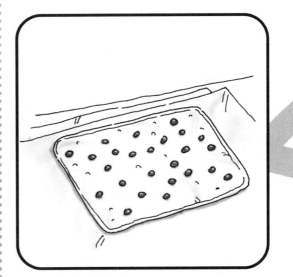

Have children set the washcloths
aside until the paint has dried.

After children have completed their projects, have
them each tell someone about Gideon's prayer and how
God answered it.

**ASK:**
● What did Gideon pray for?
● How did God answer Gideon's prayer?
● What can you pray to God about?

**BIBLE PASSAGE:**
*Judges 6:36-40; 7:16-21*

**BIBLE FOCUS:**
Obey God.

**BIBLE WORDS:**
"The Midianites ran, crying out as they fled" (Judges 7:21b).

**BIBLE STORY:**
# Gideon

ollowing God's directions, Gideon gave each of his soldiers a sword, a trumpet, and a torch hidden in a pottery jar. Then these soldiers surrounded their enemies the Midianites, blew their trumpets, smashed their jars, waved their torches in the air, and shouted, "for the Lord and for Gideon." The terrified Midianites ran away, and Gideon and his people lived in peace. Use this craft to help preschoolers act out Gideon's story.

## GIDEON'S TORCH

**MATERIALS:**
For each child, you will need the following:

● Paper towel tube
● One ½-inch Styrofoam ball
● Red craft paint and a brush
● Red and orange craft feathers
● Craft glue

# How to make "Gideon's Torch"

**1**

Have children each paint a Styrofoam ball red and allow it to dry.

**2**

Have each child glue the Styrofoam ball onto one end of a paper towel tube.

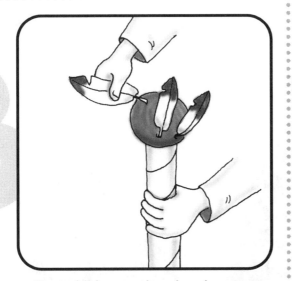

**3**

Have children push red and orange feathers, in random order, into the Styrofoam balls, covering them to create the "flames" of the torch.

**4**

Have children wave their torches in the air and shout, "for the Lord and for Gideon."

After your preschoolers have completed their torches, have them act out the story by waving their torches in the air and shouting, "for the Lord and for Gideon," as they march around the room.

## ASK:

- How do you think the soldiers felt as they surrounded their enemies?
- If you were one of Gideon's soldiers, how do think you would've felt when you saw the Midianites run away?
- How do you think God feels when you obey him and follow his directions?

## BIBLE PASSAGES:
*1 Kings 17:1-6;*
*2 Kings 2:11-12*

## BIBLE FOCUS:
God cares for us.

## BIBLE WORDS:
"The ravens brought him bread and meat in the morning and bread and meat in the evening, and he drank from the brook" (1 Kings 17:6).

## BIBLE STORY:
# Elijah

The nation of Israel was worshipping Baal and following an evil king. God announced through his prophet Elijah that he had sentenced the land to drought and famine because the people had broken their covenant with him. Yet God hid Elijah and provided water from the brook and food delivered twice daily by ravens. Use this craft to make ravens that can deliver "food" to Elijah.

# FED BY RAVENS

## MATERIALS:
For each child, you will need the following:

● Two plastic spoons (preferably black or dark in color)

● One small marble or pebble or tightly rolled piece of bread

● Black electrical tape

● One paper plate

● Tape

NOTE: Before class, cut the plate in half. One semicircle will be the wings. Cut the second semicircle into three equal wedges.

OPTIONAL: Paint the paper plates black.

**26** I Can Make It Myself!

# How to make "Fed by Ravens"

Help children tape one wedge to the back of the wings to form the bird's tail.

Now help children place the marble between the two spoon bowls.

Give each child a piece of electrical tape, and have him or her wrap it around the handles of the spoons.

Now have children tape the wings onto the handles of the spoons.

After children have completed their ravens, have them fly the birds across the room to deliver the food to Elijah.

**ASK:**
- How did God provide food for Elijah?
- How do you think Elijah felt when his meals were specially delivered?
- How does God provide food for you?

## BIBLE PASSAGES:
*1 Kings 17:1-6;*
*2 Kings 2:11-12*

## BIBLE FOCUS:
God took Elijah
to heaven.

## BIBLE WORDS:
"Elijah went up to
heaven in a whirlwind"
(2 Kings 2:11b).

# Elijah

**E**lijah was one of two people mentioned in the Bible who went to heaven without dying. Instead, Elijah went to heaven in a whirlwind! Elijah was one of God's prophets, who received messages from God to tell his people. Use this craft to let your children imagine a whirlwind.

## MATERIALS:
For each child, you will
need the following:

● Paper

● Tempera paint
(watered down) in
fire colors like red,
orange, and yellow.
(Alternatives to paint
could be markers.
The effect would look
more like a tornado.
With markers, the
pin and magazine
are optional.)

● Straws

● Crayons or a sticker
of a man

● Cardboard pieces
or magazines

● Pin

● Paint smocks (optional)
The paint shouldn't
spatter too much
because only a small
amount is used, but
some children like the
security of a smock.

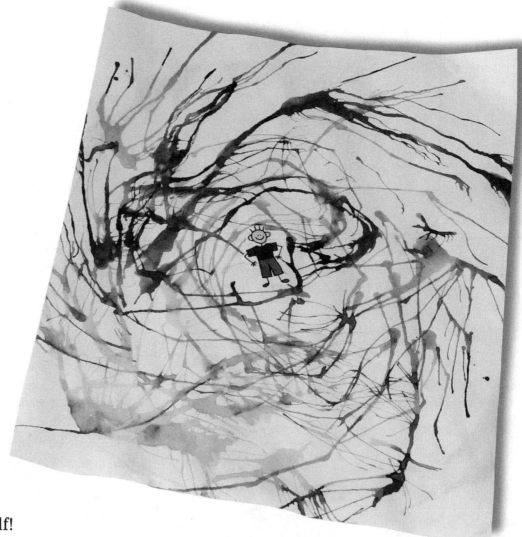

# TO HEAVEN
# IN A WHIRLWIND

# How to make "To Heaven in a Whirlwind"

Have children work with a partner. Have each pair put a paper on a piece of cardboard or a magazine. An adult should insert a pushpin in the middle so the paper will spin around.

Have children drop a few watery globs of paint onto the paper.

Have one child blow the paint with a straw while the partner spins the paper. To make a new picture, have partners trade jobs after the first person has finished blowing.

When the paint has dried, have children add a sticker of a man or draw an outline of Elijah in the whirlwind.

After the children have completed their whirlwind pictures, let them act out a whirlwind by spinning around on command. Remind them that Elijah gave important messages from God before he was taken to heaven in a whirlwind. Let them say something like "God loves you" while spinning around.

## ASK:

- How do you think Elijah felt when he was in the whirlwind going up to heaven?
- How did you feel spinning around like a whirlwind?
- How do you think Elijah felt when he got up to heaven to see God?
- What do you think heaven will be like?

**BIBLE FOCUS:**
Daniel stayed true
to God.

**BIBLE WORDS:**
"The guard took away
their choice food and
the wine they were to
drink and gave them
vegetables instead"
(Daniel 1:16).

**BIBLE STORY:**

# Daniel

**D**aniel could not eat the food from the king's table and still please God, so he politely spoke to the official and convinced him to let him eat more healthy vegetables. Daniel stayed healthy eating the vegetables. Use this craft to talk about healthy vegetables that Daniel may have eaten.

## VEGETABLES ANYONE?

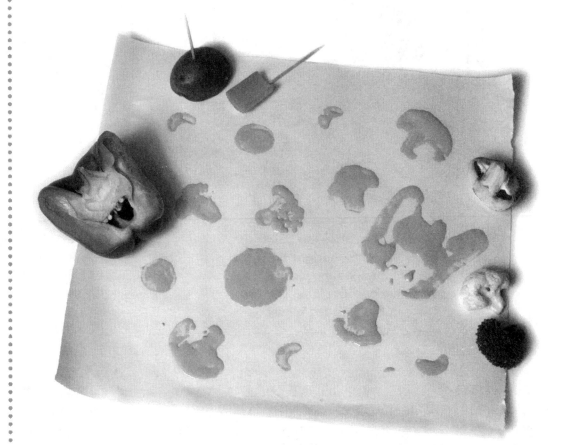

**MATERIALS:**
For this craft, you will
need the following:

● Assorted cut-up
  vegetables like celery
  stalks, carrot sticks,
  potato halves, green
  pepper halves, mush-
  rooms, and broccoli

● Toothpicks for
  the vegetables

● Marshmallow crème
  thinned with water
  and colored with
  several different
  food colors

● Paper plates

● Newsprint

# How to make "Vegetables Anyone?"

Before children arrive, gather an assortment of cut-up vegetables and prepare the marshmallow crème mixtures on paper plates.

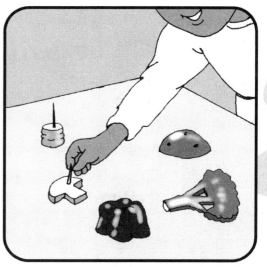

To make printing easier, have children stick toothpicks into all the vegetables.

Have children dip their vegetable into the colored crème and make a print on paper.

Encourage children to share different vegetables and different colors to create their own designs. Then they can enjoy tasting the vegetables!

Start the painting part of the project right away. While the prints dry, tell the story about Daniel and ask the questions below. Children can use the papers for wrapping paper or as a picture.

**ASK:**
- How do you think Daniel felt when he was told he could not eat the food God wanted him to eat?
- What are some of your favorite vegetables to eat?
- Why is it important to eat healthy things instead of just candy?

## BIBLE PASSAGE:
*Daniel: 1:1-16; 6*

## BIBLE FOCUS:
God helps us when we're afraid.

## BIBLE WORDS:
"God...shut the mouths of the lions" (Daniel 6:22).

## BIBLE STORY:
# Daniel

**D**aniel worshipped God even when his life was in danger. He believed that his God would protect him from anything that men could do to him. God demonstrated his protection by shutting the lions' mouths and keeping Daniel safe throughout the long night. Because of Daniel's faith, others began to worship God. Use this craft to help your little ones act out the protection of God in shutting the lions' mouths.

# SHUTTING THE LIONS' MOUTHS

## MATERIALS:
For each child, you will need the following:

- Two berry baskets spray painted brown
- Two chenille wires
- Two 6-inch pieces of yarn
- Two construction paper ears already cut out
- 6x3-inch piece of yellow construction paper for the mane
- Three large black pompoms for nose and eyes
- Glue stick

# How to make "Shutting the Lions' Mouths"

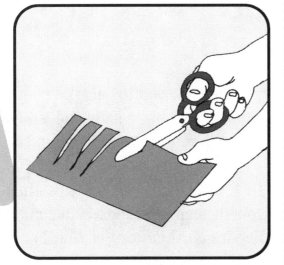

Before class, cut fringe into the yellow paper so that it looks like a mane.

Using two 6-inch pieces of yarn, help children tie the baskets together in two places.

Have children glue the eyes and nose to the top front portion of the basket. Glue the mane to the top of the basket, and glue the ears behind the mane.

Now have children make whiskers by each bending two chenille wires and threading them through the berry basket under the lion's nose.

After children have completed their lions, have them use the lions to act out the story of Daniel in the lions' den.

**ASK:**
- How do you think Daniel felt when he was thrown into the lions' den?
- What are some things that you are afraid of?
- How do you feel knowing that God will protect you when you are afraid?

**BIBLE PASSAGE:**
*Daniel 3*

**BIBLE FOCUS:**
God protects us.

**BIBLE WORDS:**
"God...has sent his angel and rescued his servants!" (Daniel 3:28b).

# Shadrach, Meshach, and Abednego

**K**ing Nebuchadnezzar of Babylon wanted all the people in his kingdom to bow down and worship a giant golden statue. But Shadrach, Meshach, and Abednego refused to bow down because they worshipped only God. Although the furious king threw the three men into a fiery furnace, he let them go when he saw them walking around unharmed with a fourth man who looked like an angel. Use this craft to help preschoolers retell this story of God's protection.

## FIERY FURNACE VIEWER

**MATERIALS:**

For each child, you will need the following:

- 8x10-inch cardboard mat with a 5x7-inch opening
- 6½x8-inch piece of cardboard backing
- 6½x8-inch piece of red cellophane
- 5½x8-inch piece of card stock
- Masking tape
- Black marker

NOTE: You can purchase ready-made mats at craft stores. Or to make your own, cut a 5x7-inch opening in the center of an 8x10-inch piece of cardboard, leaving a 1½-inch mat border on all four sides.

**34**   I Can Make It Myself!

# How to make the "Fiery Furnace Viewer"

**1.** Before children arrive, tape the cellophane onto the back of each mat, covering the opening.

**2.** Help children tape three sides of the cardboard, leaving one of the 6½-inch sides open on the back of the mat to create a sleeve.

**3.** The children will draw Shadrach, Meshach, Abednego, and an angel on a piece of card stock.
Note: Younger preschoolers will need assistance from an adult.

**4.** Have children insert the card stock picture-side up into the cardboard sleeve.

After your preschoolers have completed their sliding viewers, have them slide the card stock far enough to see only Shadrach, Meshach, and Abednego, keeping the angel covered. Then have preschoolers slide the card stock to reveal the angel and say, "Praise God! He sent an angel to save us from the fire."

**ASK:**

● How do you think Shadrach, Meshach, and Abednego felt when they were thrown into the fiery furnace?

● How do you think they felt when they saw the angel in the fire with them?

● What are some ways that God protects us?

*Shadrach, Meshach, and Abednego*  **35**

**BIBLE FOCUS:**
God never leaves us.

**BIBLE WORDS:**
"He said, 'Look! I see four men walking around in the fire, unbound and unharmed, and the fourth looks like a son of the gods'" (Daniel 3:25).

**BIBLE STORY:**

# Shadrach, Meshach, and Abednego

Shadrach, Meshach, and Abednego refused to compromise their faithfulness to God by bowing to Nebuchadnezzar's golden image—even though it meant certain death in Nebuchadnezzar's furnace. God demonstrated his absolute power, presence, and protection within the fiery furnace as Nebuchadnezzar watched four men walk safely among the flames. Help your little ones recreate the scene with this craft and remember that God will be there for them, too.

# IN THE FURNACE

**MATERIALS:**
- For teacher, cool glue gun.

For each child, you will need the following:

- A clear plastic or glass jar with a wide mouth
- Four small wooden or plastic figures
- Water and glycerin combination (one teaspoon glycerin per one cup water) or water only
- Red glitter or small red metallic confetti
- Glue
- A small pitcher

# How to make "In the Furnace"

An adult will need to help the children glue the four figures onto the bottom of the inside of each jar.

When the glue has dried, help children fill the jars almost to the top with the water and glycerin mixture.

Now have children add the red glitter or confetti to the jars.

Finally, have children glue the lids onto the jars.

After your children have completed their crafts, let them shake the jars to see the four men safe inside the fiery furnace.

**ASK:**
- Why didn't Shadrach, Meshach, and Abednego bow to the king's statue?
- How do you think they felt when their ropes fell away and God's angel was walking safely inside with them?
- Is there ever any time that God is not with you?

*Shadrach, Meshach, and Abednego*  **37**

**BIBLE PASSAGE:**
*1 Samuel 16:1-13; 17*

**BIBLE FOCUS:**
God looks at our hearts.

**BIBLE WORDS:**
"The Lord does not look at the things man looks at. Man looks at the outward appearance, but the Lord looks at the heart" (1 Samuel 16:7b).

**BIBLE STORY:**
# David

God sent Samuel to anoint a new king among Jesse's sons. Samuel met each of Jesse's older sons, and though they were strong, handsome, and accomplished, God did not choose any of them. God had chosen David, Jesse's youngest son, who was out tending the sheep. God chose David because God knew what was in David's heart. Use this craft to help children learn that God cares most about what we're like on the inside.

# IN YOUR HEART T-SHIRTS

**MATERIALS:**

For each child, you will need the following:

● A clean white T-shirt, washed, dried (without fabric softener), and pressed

● Packets of unsweetened drink mix in several colors

● White vinegar

● Small bowls

● Cotton swabs

● A black fabric marker

● Cardboard

● Plastic garbage bags

● Scissors

● Rubber bands

# How to make "In Your Heart T-Shirts"

Mix each packet of drink mix with a quarter cup of white vinegar in a small bowl.

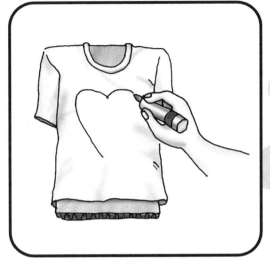

Have children insert a piece of cardboard into their T-shirts. Then have them each draw a large heart on the front of their shirts.

An adult will need to cover the children's clothes with plastic garbage bags.

Have children paint the hearts with colors and add shapes that represent things they like to do or characteristics of themselves. Then set aside the T-shirts to dry.

*NOTE: When the shirts are completely dry, press them using a pressing cloth. Let the shirts sit for ten hours. Wash shirts on gentle cycle in cold water and tumble dry.*

When the children have finished making their T-shirts, tell them the story of how David was anointed king. Talk about 1 Samuel 16:7. Remind them that God knows their hearts and loves them very much.

## ASK:
- Why does God care about what we're like on the inside?
- What are you like on the inside?
- What does God see in your heart?

## BIBLE PASSAGE:
*1 Samuel 16:1-13; 17*

## BIBLE FOCUS:
Even small people can do big things.

## BIBLE WORDS:
"So David triumphed over the Philistine with a sling and a stone; without a sword in his hand he struck down the Philistine and killed him" (1 Samuel 17:50).

## BIBLE STORY:
# David

The story of David and Goliath is a classic that children love. They love to hear how the young boy David defeated the terrible giant that frightened all of Saul's soldiers. Use this craft to help young children act out the story of little David versus big Goliath.

# A BIG GUY AND A LITTLE GUY

## MATERIALS:
For each child, you will need the following:

● A white tube sock

● A white crew sock

● A Styrofoam cup with the bottom cut out

● Several rubber bands

● Markers

● Dry rice, beans, or peas

● A sharp pair of scissors (for adult use only)

**40** I Can Make It Myself!

# How to make "A Big Guy and a Little Guy"

Have children fill both socks three-quarters full with beans, rice, or peas. The tube sock will become Goliath; the crew sock will become David.

The children need to use rubber bands to close off the top of the socks so the beans don't fall out, and to form the noses on both figures.

An adult should cut down the middle of the leftover length of sock. Have children arrange the fabric to look like a headdress. If you like, you can add a thick rubber band to hold the "headdress" in place.

Have children use markers to create faces and to decorate the bodies on both figures.

After children have finished making the sock puppets, have them use the figures to act out the story of David and Goliath.

## ASK:
● David is little compared with Goliath. How did David win?

● What do you think the rest of the Philistines thought when they saw that Goliath was defeated?
● What do you think the rest of Saul's army thought when they saw that David had won?
● How does God help you with the tough things you have to do?

**BIBLE PASSAGE:**
*Esther 3–5*

**BIBLE FOCUS:**
God works in our lives.

**BIBLE WORDS:**
"In all things God works for the good of those who love him" (Romans 8:28).

**BIBLE STORY:**

## Queen Esther

**E**sther risked her life to approach the king with her plea to save the Israelite people. By extending his golden scepter to Esther, the king indicated that he would spare Esther's life, even though by approaching him uninvited she could have been sentenced to death. Use this craft to help your preschoolers act out Esther's courage and God's provision.

# THE KING'S SCEPTER

**MATERIALS:**
For each child, you will need the following:

- One paper towel tube (or section of gift-wrap tube)
- Two 10-ounce Styrofoam cups
- Gold spray paint
- Selection of glitter, sequins, plastic craft "jewels," or metallic confetti
- Glue

# How to make "The King's Scepter"

Before class, spray gold paint on the paper towel tubes and Styrofoam cups.

Help children glue the bottom of one cup to one end of the paper towel tube.

Then help them glue a second cup to the mouth of the first one.

Glue decorations to the cup to look like jewels.

After children have completed their scepters, have them act out the story of Esther's courage.

## ASK:
- How do you think Esther felt when she walked into the king's room?
- Why did she do it?
- How did God use Esther to take care of her people?
- How does God use other people to help take care of us?

**BIBLE PASSAGE:**
*Esther 3-5*

**BIBLE FOCUS:**
God protects me.

**BIBLE WORDS:**
"The Lord...will strengthen and protect you" (2 Thessalonians 3:3).

**BIBLE STORY:**

# Queen Esther

**W**hen the Jewish people in Persia were faced with destruction, God raised up Esther to be queen. King Xerxes did not know that Esther, whom he had chosen to be his queen, was a Jew. At the risk of her own life, Esther stood before the king and pleaded on behalf of her people. God protected Esther and through her bravery saved the Jewish people. To act out the story, this crown can be used for either Xerxes or Esther and can help the children remember how God protected this brave queen.

# ESTHER'S CROWNS

**MATERIALS:**

For each child, you will need the following:

- One 3-pound butter tub, or 12-ounce frozen topping tub
- Glue
- Aluminum foil
- An assortment of decorative trims, beads, and stickers

# How to make "Esther's Crowns"

Before children arrive, cut out the base of the butter tubs and scallop the edges.

Have children cover their crowns with aluminum foil.

Have children glue on ribbon or trim.

Have kids add shiny stickers and bright beads.

Esther's crown identified her as royalty, but her brave deeds proved that her heart trusted in God. Talk about Esther's faith and courage.

**ASK:**
- How was Esther brave?
- How did God protect Esther?
- How does God protect you?

**BIBLE FOCUS:**
God cares for us.

**BIBLE WORDS:**
"The Lord provided a great fish to swallow Jonah" (Jonah 1:17).

**BIBLE STORY:**

# Jonah and the Big Fish

God told Jonah to go to Nineveh. But Jonah ran away from God on a boat. When the sea grew rough, Jonah told the other sailors to toss him into the ocean and the sea would be calm again. God took care of Jonah by providing a big fish to swallow him. He was in the fish for three days and nights. God made the fish spit Jonah onto dry land. Use this fish-toss game craft to show your little ones that God took care of Jonah.

## IN THE BELLY OF THE BIG FISH

**MATERIALS:**
For each child, you will need the following:

● A clean, empty milk jug
● 2-foot piece of string
● Large bead
● Glue stick
● Construction paper fish tail
● Crayons

# How to make "In the Belly of the Big Fish"

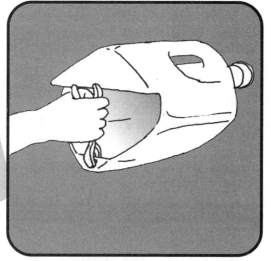

Before children arrive, cut mouthlike holes in the large end of the milk jugs and use a hole punch to punch a hole near the bottom edge of each mouth.

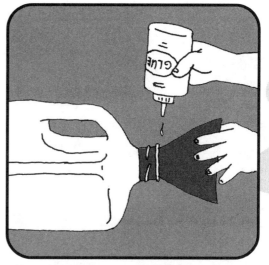

Have children glue the fish tail to the small end of the milk jug.

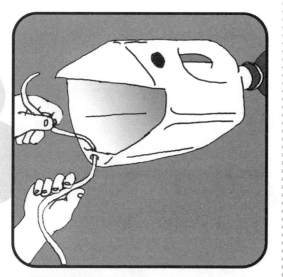

Help each child thread one end of the string through the hole in the fish's mouth and tie it in a knot.

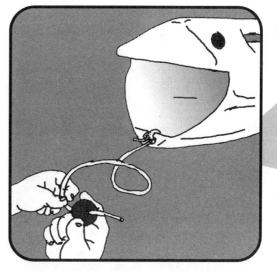

Help each child thread the other end of the string through the hole in the bead and tie it in a knot. Children may use crayons to decorate their fish and beads if they wish.

After children have completed their fish-toss game craft, have them play the game by trying to catch the bead with the fish. They can act out the story of Jonah and the big fish, pretending the bead is Jonah.

**ASK:**
- How do you think Jonah felt in the belly of the big fish?
- Think of a time when God took care of you, and tell it to a friend.
- How does God take care of you?

**BIBLE PASSAGE:**
*Jonah 1–4*

**BIBLE FOCUS:**
God saves us.

**BIBLE WORDS:**
"Salvation comes from the Lord" (Jonah 2:9b).

**BIBLE STORY:**

# Jonah and the Big Fish

**A**s Jonah ran away from God, a violent storm arose, putting the boat that Jonah was on in great danger. Jonah knew that the storm was from God, so he asked the sailors to throw him overboard. The raging sea grew still, and Jonah was saved in the belly of a big fish.

# STUCK ON JONAH

**MATERIALS:**
For each child, you will need the following:

● Two 8½x11-inch pieces of blue vinyl (from fabric store, or use clear vinyl and blue plastic wrap)

● White dot stickers

● Green, pink, and gray construction paper

● Crayons or marker pens

# How to make "Stuck on Jonah"

**1** Before children arrive, cut the pink construction paper into simple people shapes, and cut the gray construction paper into large fish shapes.

**2** Have each child put a fish and a Jonah figure on one piece of the vinyl. They may add facial features to Jonah and the fish.

**3** Have children rip green construction paper and place it on the vinyl to make seaweed. Have them stick white dots on the vinyl for air bubbles.

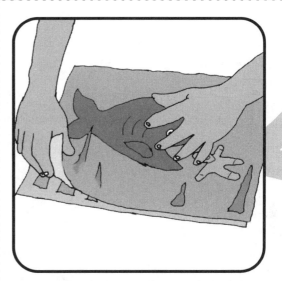

**4** Have children place the second piece of vinyl over the Jonah scene and rub firmly around the paper pieces, so the two pieces of vinyl stick together.

After children have completed their Jonah ocean scenes, have them stick their vinyl picture to a window by rubbing it against the glass. Let them retell the story while opening up the vinyl pieces and moving Jonah around.

## ASK:
- How do you think Jonah felt inside the big fish?
- How did God save Jonah?
- What do you think Jonah looked like after the fish spit him out?
- How does God save us?

**BIBLE PASSAGE:**

*Matthew 1:18-25;*
*Luke 1:26–2:21*

**BIBLE FOCUS:**

We should share
God's love.

**BIBLE WORDS:**

"God [is] with us"
(Matthew 1:23b).

**G**od sent his only Son for all of us, showing God's great love for us. God's love is something that we can share with others. What better way to help children share than with a Christmas present that they give to someone else?

# CHRISTMAS PRESENT

**MATERIALS:**

For each child, you will
need the following:

● Paper towel tube

● Wrapping paper

● Ribbon or
  pipe cleaners

● Tape

● Candy (Alternatives
  to candy could be
  Christmas pictures
  the children have
  colored, a bag of
  cereals that the class
  has mixed together, a
  bag of popcorn
  they've popped, or an
  invitation to come to
  church with them.)

● Tags that read,
  "Share God's Love
  for Christmas."
  (Each should have
  a hole punched in
  one corner.)

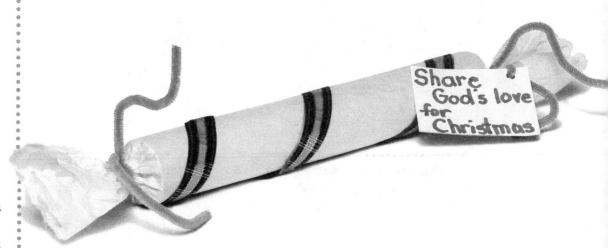

# How to make "Christmas Present"

1

Have children slide candy pieces
or other gifts into empty tubes.

2

Have kids roll their tubes in wrapping
paper and tape the middle.

3

Help children gather the ends
with ribbon or pipe cleaners.

4

To finish the project, help children
attach the tags to one pipe cleaner
or to a piece of ribbon.

Tell the story of Christmas, and talk about Jesus being
a gift to everyone. Have children bring their gifts to a
pretend baby Jesus and tell him why they have
brought a present.

**ASK:**
- What kinds of gifts does God give us?
- How do you feel when you get a gift?
- To whom could you give this Christmas present?

## BIBLE PASSAGES:

*Matthew 1:18-25;*
*Luke 1:26–2:21*

## BIBLE FOCUS:

The birth of Jesus is a reason to celebrate.

## BIBLE WORDS:

"Today in the town of David a Savior has been born to you; he is Christ the Lord" (Luke 2:11).

# Birth of Jesus

**T**wo thousand years ago in a small stable, a tiny, perfect baby boy was born. That boy grew up and was called Wonderful Counselor, Mighty God, Everlasting Father, and Prince of Peace. He was also called Immanuel, Christ, and Savior. Jesus' birth is worthy of a tremendous celebration. Use this craft to help preschoolers celebrate the birth of Jesus.

# CELEBRATION SUN-CATCHERS

## MATERIALS:

For each child, you will need the following:

- A plastic lid, from a container like a cottage cheese tub
- School glue gel
- Flat evergreen sprig
- Craft sticks
- Bits and pieces of Christmas art supplies such as curling ribbon, Christmas tissue paper, and glitter (Choose items that look the same on both sides. For example, you wouldn't want to use wrapping paper that's only colored on one side.)

# How to make "Celebration Sun-Catchers"

Have children spread a thin layer of glue gel on the inside surface of the plastic lids and spread the glue with craft sticks.

Have kids arrange the evergreen sprigs and the other items on top of the glue.

Finally have children completely cover the evergreen sprigs and the other items with more glue gel.

When the glue has dried, help children pop the sun-catchers out of the lids. An adult will need to use a skewer to poke a hole in the top of each sun-catcher, thread a ribbon through the hole, and tie the ends.

*NOTE: It will take the glue two to four days to dry. If you need to send the ornaments home before they've dried, explain to the children's parents how to attach the ribbon to the top so children can hang the ornaments. Hold the wet ornaments flat. You may cover the glue with plastic wrap, but tell parents to remove it when they get home.*

While the children work on their sun-catchers, talk about celebrating Jesus' birth at Christmas. Tell the children that for many years, people looked forward to Jesus' birth, and they celebrated when he was finally born.

## ASK:

● Why do we celebrate Christmas?

● Why is Jesus' birthday such a good thing?

● How do you celebrate Christmas at your house?

**BIBLE PASSAGES:**
*Matthew 4:18-22;*
*Mark 1:16-20*

**BIBLE FOCUS:**
Follow Jesus!

**BIBLE WORDS:**
"Come, follow me"
(Matthew 4:19a).

# Jesus Calls His Disciples

**A** disciple is a special follower of Jesus who tells other people about God. This is how Jesus called his disciples: Jesus was walking beside the Sea of Galilee when he saw Simon and his brother Andrew fishing. Jesus said, "Come, follow me, and I will make you fishers of men." Make this beautiful picture to remind your kids to follow Jesus.

## A BRUSH WITH GREATNESS

**MATERIALS:**
For each child, you will need the following:

● Copies of the reproducible boat on page 94

● Tape

● Paper

● Sidewalk chalk

● Tissues

# How to make "A Brush With Greatness"

Before children arrive, tape the reproducible boat pictures to the table.

Have children rip the top of a plain sheet of paper in a wavy line.

Have kids rub chalk on the ripped edge.

With a tissue, have children brush the chalk off onto the boat picture. Repeat this step, moving the ripped page down each time.

After you have made your brushed chalk pictures,

**ASK:**
- What did the disciples do when Jesus said, "Follow me?"
- How can you follow Jesus?
- How can you tell others about Jesus?

## BIBLE PASSAGES:
*Matthew 4:18-22;*
*Mark 1:16-20*

## BIBLE FOCUS:
We should bring others to God.

## BIBLE WORDS:
"I will make you fishers of men" (Matthew 4:19b).

# Jesus Calls His Disciples

Jesus called fishermen to leave familiar nets and waters to join him in gathering people to God. Use this craft to make a reminder that we are still called to be "fishers of men."

# FISHERS OF MEN

## MATERIALS:
For each child, you will need the following:

- One 15x20-inch rectangle of light colored (white or ecru) fabric
- One dry cleaners' pants hanger
- One very scaly fish purchased from a market, or a plastic fish with pronounced scales
- Fabric paint
- Fabric markers
- One shallow tray
- One paintbrush or small paint roller
- Masking tape
- Craft stick or rubber glove

**56** I Can Make It Myself!

# How to make "Fishers of Men"

Before class, use the fabric markers to write, "Fishers of Men" across the top of each fabric rectangle. Be sure to allow about an inch to attach to the hanger. Place a thin, shallow layer of paint in the tray.

Have children use a paintbrush to cover one side of their fish with a thin layer of paint.

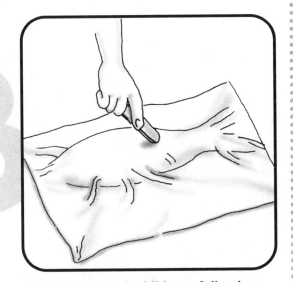

Now have each child carefully place the fabric onto the painted side of the fish and rub the back of the fabric with a craft stick or finger.

Finally have children carefully peel the fabric away from the fish. Repeat steps two through four if desired.

After your children have completed the prints, make the banners by using masking tape to attach the children's prints to the cardboard tubes on dry cleaners' pants hangers.

When you've finished the banners,

**ASK:**
- What do fishermen do?
- What does it mean to be "fishers of men"?
- How can we work today as fishers of men for Jesus?

# The Sermon on the Mount

**BIBLE PASSAGES:**
*Matthew 5:13-16; 6:19-21; Luke 12:33-34*

**BIBLE FOCUS:**
God wants us to spread his Word and love all over the world.

**BIBLE WORDS:**
"You are the salt of the earth" (Matthew 5:13a).

Jesus had important rules he wanted people to know about. He told people about the rules through what we call the Sermon on the Mount. Use this craft to help children see how quickly God's Word can spread to other people and how they can help spread God's Word and become "salt and light."

# SALT AND LIGHT

**MATERIALS:**

For each child, you will need the following:

- One clear 6x6-inch square of self-adhesive paper (You will need to remove the backing and place the paper on a table with the sticky side up.)

- Blue construction paper

- Salt shakers

- Watercolor paints

- Water cups to dilute paint

- A spray bottle of water (children can share this)

- A stapler (children can share one)

# How to make "Salt and Light"

Have children sprinkle salt all over the sticky side of a piece of self-adhesive paper.

Have children use watercolors to paint or drop paint onto the salted paper.

Now have children gently mist the finished painting. (This will fuse the colors together.)

Have an adult staple the four corners of the salt painting onto a blue piece of paper and write, "Salt and Light" on the background paper.

Talk about how one drop of color could spread so fast and how it could mix with the other drops of color.

**ASK:**
- What happened when you sprayed the water on your picture?
- How is this like spreading God's love?
- How can you help spread God's love all around?

**BIBLE FOCUS:**
God gives treasures.

**BIBLE WORDS:**
"Store up for yourselves treasures in heaven" (Matthew 6:20a).

**BIBLE STORY:**

# The Sermon on the Mount

Jesus reminds his followers that earthly treasures do not last, but heavenly treasures remain forever. This craft will help children name several "treasures" God gives to us and associate those treasures with symbols of God's great love.

# TREASURE JAR

**MATERIALS:**

For each child, you will need the following:

- Baby food jar with lid
- ¾ cup uncooked rice
- Small scoop
- Small symbols of God's gifts to us such as a rainbow eraser, heart bead, seashell, Jesus sticker adhered to poster board, cross, angel, dove, etc.

# How to make the "Treasure Jar"

Have children scoop rice into a
jar until it is half full.

Inside the jar, have them place
five or six small symbols of
"heavenly treasures."

Next have kids add rice to the
jar until it is nearly full. Seal the jar
with a tight-fitting lid.

Show each child how to turn or shake
the jar to reveal the hidden symbols.
Help him or her name the symbols and
explain what they might mean.

After children complete the treasure jars,

**ASK:**
- What does it feel like to find a treasure?
- How does God's love make you feel?
- What treasures do you see in your treasure jar that
  make you think of treasures from God?

**BIBLE PASSAGE:**
Matthew 7:24-27

**BIBLE FOCUS:**
Disobedience isn't wise.

**BIBLE WORDS:**
"But everyone who hears these words of mine and does not put them into practice is like a foolish man who built his house on sand" (Matthew 7:26).

**BIBLE STORY:**

# Wise and Foolish Builders

**T**his parable, which comes at the end of the Sermon on the Mount, encourages us to listen carefully to Jesus' teachings, to carefully obey them, and to build our lives on the foundation of God. Jesus knew that building a life based on obedience is the best way to weather the storms of life. Use this craft to help your preschoolers learn that disobeying God isn't a very good idea.

## HOUSE ON THE SAND

**MATERIALS:**
For each child, you will need the following:

- A clear plastic cup
- A sugar cube
- One tablespoon of the following mixture: Mix one packet unsweetened lemonade mix with one cup of brown sugar.
- One-half to two-thirds cup of water
- A plastic spoon

# How to make the "House on the Sand"

Have each child add one tablespoon of the lemonade mix to his or her cup. Explain that this mix is the sand.

Have each child place a sugar cube on top of the lemonade mix in his or her cup. Explain that this is the house.

Have each child add one-half to two-thirds cup water to the cup. Explain that this is the rain.

Have each child stir the lemonade until the sugar dissolves.

After children have stirred the mixtures in their cups, ask them what they observe about their houses—the houses have dissolved in the rainstorm. While they enjoy their lemony drink, tell children what Jesus said about building their houses on the sand. Explain that Jesus didn't really mean that their houses would wash away if they disobeyed. Jesus meant that we can get into big trouble when we disobey.

## ASK:
● Why is disobeying a bad idea?
● What really happens when we disobey?
● How can we obey?
● What does Jesus think when we obey?

**BIBLE PASSAGE:**
*Matthew 7:24-27*

**BIBLE FOCUS:**
Obedience is wise.

**BIBLE WORDS:**
"Everyone who hears these words of mine and puts them into practice is like a wise man who built his house on the rock" (Matthew 7:24).

**BIBLE STORY:**

# Wise and Foolish Builders

In this parable, which is at the end of the Sermon on the Mount, Jesus encourages us to do more than obey him. Jesus encourages us to build our lives on the foundation of right living. He's asking us to wholeheartedly follow him as devoted disciples. Use this craft to help little ones understand that obeying Jesus leads to good things.

HOUSE ON THE ROCK

**MATERIALS:**
For each child, you will need the following:

- A fist-sized rock
- Self-hardening clay
- Small sticky notes
- Flat toothpicks
- Scissors

# How to make the "House on the Rock"

Have children each make a
small house out of clay.

Have each child place the house on top
of the rock and then push down slightly
so the clay sticks to the rock.

Have kids make flags by folding
sticky notes cut in half over toothpicks.

Have kids stick the flags on
the roofs of their houses.

Tell children about Jesus' parable. For each "obedience"
flag that children put on their houses, talk about one way
to obey. If you like, you can re-enact the parable by sprin-
kling water from a watering can on top of the houses.

## ASK:
- Why is it good to obey God?
- What can you do to obey God?
- What happens when you obey God?

## BIBLE PASSAGES:
*Matthew 8:23-27;*
*Mark 4:37-41;*
*Luke 8:22-25*

## BIBLE FOCUS:
Jesus is powerful.

## BIBLE WORDS:
"The winds and the waves obey him" (Matthew 8:27b).

# Jesus Calms the Storm

In the midst of a severe storm, Jesus' followers called out for him to save them. Jesus demonstrated his power by calming the winds and the waves, and his followers were amazed. Use this craft to help your little ones act out the story of the storm tossing the boat around and the power of Jesus to calm the storm.

# THE BIG BOAT

## MATERIALS:
For each child, you will need the following:

- Spring-type clothespin
- Toothpick
- 2½-inch square piece of paper
- Glue stick

# How to make "The Big Boat"

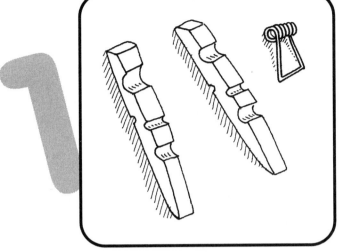

Before children arrive, separate the pieces of the clothespins and discard the springs.

Have each child glue the flat sides of two pieces of a clothespin together and then set this piece aside to dry.

Have each child make a sail by putting a toothpick in through the bottom and out through the top of the square paper.

Direct each child to attach the sail to his or her boat by putting it in the small hole from which the spring was removed.

After children have completed their boats, have them use the boats to act out the story of Jesus calming the storm.

**ASK:**
- How do you think the followers of Jesus felt during the storm?
- Have you ever felt afraid during a storm?
- What can you do if you feel afraid?

**BIBLE FOCUS:**
Jesus calms fear.

**BIBLE WORDS:**
"[Jesus] said to his disciples, 'Why are you so afraid?' " (Mark 4:40a).

**BIBLE STORY:**
# Jesus Calms the Storm

A sudden storm overtook the disciples' boat, with Jesus sleeping on board. The fearful disciples were amazed when Jesus awoke and commanded the storm to stop. This craft is designed to help children imagine the disciples' fear, as well as Jesus' ability to help them.

## STORM IN A BOTTLE

**MATERIALS:**
For each child, you will need the following:

- 20-ounce clear plastic beverage container, with cap
- 1½ cups water
- 1½ cups light corn syrup
- Blue food coloring
- Funnel
- Colorful sequin shapes (fish, stars, circles)

# How to make the "Storm in a Bottle"

**Before class, mix two drops of blue food coloring with the water.**

**Help children fill bottles with the water and corn syrup.**

**Have children place the sequins in the bottles. Then help them seal the bottles with tight-fitting caps.**

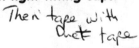

*Then tape with Duct tape*

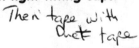

**Show each child how to shake and tip the bottle to create a stormy sea.**

After children have completed their bottles, read the Bible story to them. During the stormy part of the story, have them shake their bottles. During the end of the story, have them hold the bottles still and watch the stormy water become calm.

**ASK:**
- Who was afraid during the storm?
- What did Jesus do about the disciples' fear?
- What can you do when you feel afraid?

**BIBLE PASSAGES:**
*Matthew 13:3-10, 18-23;*
*Mark 4:3-8, 13-20;*
*Luke 8:4-8, 11-15*

**BIBLE FOCUS:**
Grow in faith.

**BIBLE WORDS:**
"Other seed fell on good soil, where it produced a crop" (Matthew 13:8a).

**BIBLE STORY:**

# The Parable of the Sower

In this Bible story, Jesus tells a parable comparing the growth of seeds with our growing understanding of God's kingdom. Those who hear God's Word and nurture it within their lives are like seeds that have fallen on good soil. This craft will remind preschoolers of Jesus' parable that encourages them to hear God's Word and live in God's love.

## SEED MAGNET

**MATERIALS:**
For each child, you will need the following:

- Masking tape
- Wax paper
- Clear-drying bottled glue (not a glue stick)
- Toothpick
- A 2-inch cookie cutter
- Dried seeds and beans (popcorn, navy beans, sunflower seeds)
- Scissors
- Magnetic tape

# How to make the "Seed Magnet"

Before class, tape the cookie cutters onto the wax paper. Have children squeeze a ⅛-inch layer of glue into the upside-down cookie cutters. Use a toothpick to evenly spread the glue.

Direct children to place seeds and beans in the glue. They'll need to press seeds down so that all are in contact with the glue.

After twenty-four hours, an adult needs to remove the wax paper and turn the cookie cutter over until the glue has completely dried (twelve to twenty-four hours). Remove the seed shape. Trim away excess glue.

Have children glue a small strip of magnetic tape to the back of the seed shape.

This craft will take two class times to complete with time for the glue to dry well between the class times. After they've completed their seed magnets, invite children to display them at home in prominent places, such as on their refrigerators.

## ASK:
- In Jesus' parable, what did the seeds need to grow strong?
- What do people need to grow strong?
- How does God help us grow strong?

**BIBLE FOCUS:**
God's words can grow
in our lives.

**BIBLE WORDS:**
"The seed is the word of
God" (Luke 8:11b).

# The Parable of the Sower

**J**esus used this parable to teach his followers that people will not respond to the gospel in the same way. He explained that Satan, persecution, peer pressure, and the desire for worldly pleasures can interfere with the seeds of truth. However, when God's Word does take root, the result is the abundant crop of a fruitful life. This activity allows your preschoolers to make a living model of this parable.

## PARABLE GARDEN

**MATERIALS:**
For each child, you will
need the following:

- A 2x2-cup section
  of an egg carton

- Potting soil

- A rock that fits
  snugly inside one
  of the egg cups

- Small weeds

- Seeds (bean or
  marigold seed
  work well)

# How to make the "Parable Garden"

Have each child very firmly press potting soil into one of the four sections of the egg carton.

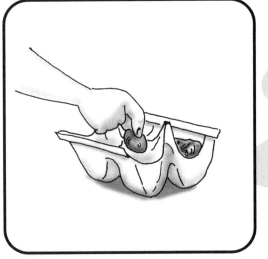

Next, have each child place a rock in one of the four sections of the egg carton and cover with a thin layer of potting soil.

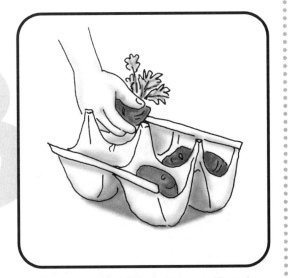

Direct each child to place soil and weeds in one section of the egg carton.

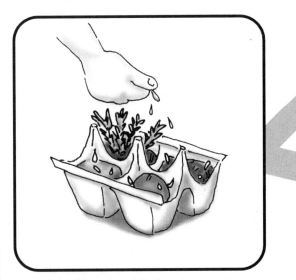

Have kids loosely fill the last sections of the egg cartons with the potting soil and sprinkle seeds over all the egg carton sections.

After kids have assembled the Parable Gardens, explain what each section of the egg carton represents from the parable. Be sure to water regularly, and place the gardens in a sunny spot.

**ASK:**
- What will the seeds in our gardens need?
- Which seeds do you think will not grow well?
- God wants good things to grow in our hearts. How can we help that happen?

**BIBLE FOCUS:**
Jesus provides for us.

**BIBLE WORDS:**
"They all ate and were satisfied" (Matthew 14:20a).

**BIBLE STORY:**

# Jesus Feeds Thousands

Though Jesus tried to find time to be alone, the crowds followed him. The people were so eager to encounter Jesus, that they stayed all day in a remote place where there was no food. The disciples encouraged Jesus to send the crowd away so they might find food. Instead, Jesus miraculously fed them all. Use this craft to help your preschoolers see that from five loaves and two fish, Jesus fed 5,000 people until they were full.

## TWELVE BASKETS

**MATERIALS:**
For each child, you will need the following:

- One large biscuit of shredded wheat cereal
- White glue, slightly diluted with water
- A plastic bowl
- A few oyster crackers
- A few goldfish crackers
- A sheet of wax paper

# How to make the "Twelve Baskets"

Have children crumble the
biscuits into the bowls.

Add diluted white glue to the
bowls. Have children mix the wheat
and the glue together—the
mixture should be thick.

Have children each form a ball
with the shredded wheat mixture and
use their thumbs to make a center
indentation—this method is similar
to making a pinch pot.

At the appropriate time in the story,
have children add a few oyster crackers
and goldfish crackers to their baskets to
represent the loaves and the fish.

Leave the baskets on the table, and gather the children
in another area. Tell them the story, and pass out oyster
crackers and goldfish crackers at the appropriate time.
Then have the children act as the disciples did by going
over to the table and carefully bringing the baskets
back to the story area. Have children look inside all of
the baskets to see how much food was left over.

## ASK:
● How do you think Jesus turned five loaves and two
fish into enough food to feed all those people?
● Why do you think Jesus provided food for them
to eat?
● How does Jesus provide for your needs?

**BIBLE PASSAGE:**
*Matthew 14:13-21*

**BIBLE FOCUS:**
Jesus loves people.

**BIBLE WORDS:**
"When Jesus landed and saw a large crowd, he had compassion on them and healed their sick" (Matthew 14:14).

# Jesus Feeds Thousands

Though Jesus craved solitude, his love for people compelled him to set aside his own needs to heal them, teach them, and provide for them. Jesus' miraculous ability to create food for more than 5,000 should give the preschoolers in your class confidence that Jesus cares for them and will generously provide for them.

## JESUS CARES FOR PEOPLE

**MATERIALS:**
For each child, you will need the following:

- Construction paper
- Unwrapped crayon
- Rice
- Glue
- Marker

# How to make "Jesus Cares for People"

Before children arrive, spread a thin layer of glue on at least one sheet of paper. Sprinkle a generous amount of rice on the glue, and allow the glue to dry.

Draw Jesus with five loaves of bread and two fish. Photocopy the drawing onto construction paper. You'll need one copy for each child.

Have children put the pictures with the drawing on top of the paper with the rice glued to it. Have kids rub the crayons on the paper to create their rubbings.

Have children each add a drawing of themselves to their pictures.

As children create their pictures, tell them the story of Jesus feeding thousands. As you hand out the photocopy of the drawing to each child, tell kids about how Jesus needed to feed the people who had come to him. To find out how many people Jesus fed, have the children make rubbings as indicated in the instructions. Each mark left by the rice represents a person that Jesus fed that day. Talk about how Jesus loves them and provides for them every day.

## ASK:

● What is the biggest number you know?
● Could Jesus feed that many people?
● Why would Jesus want to feed all those people?
● Why does Jesus want to take care of us?

**BIBLE PASSAGE:**
*Luke 15:11-24*

**BIBLE FOCUS:**
Our Father, God, loves us always.

**BIBLE WORDS:**
"He ran to his son, threw his arms around him and kissed him" (Luke 15:20b).

# The Prodigal Son

**A**n unwise son went to his father and asked for his inheritance. The father gave him a large amount of money, which the son quickly spent on foolish living. Then, poor and hungry, the son returned to his father, hoping to work as a servant. But the father received him with a hug of love and forgiveness, welcoming his son back into the family. Use this craft to teach about God's unconditional love for us.

## THE FATHER'S HUG

**MATERIALS:**
For each child, you will need the following:

- A 4-foot length of paper
- Scissors
- Crayons or marker pens
- Heart stickers

**78** I Can Make It Myself!

# How to make "The Father's Hug"

Have each child find a partner. Have one child lie down, with arms straight out, on a 4-foot length of heavy paper, while the other child outlines only his or her arms. Switch roles so each child has a drawing.

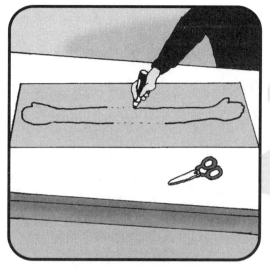

Have children draw lines to connect the two arms.

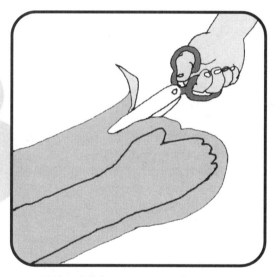

Help children cut out the arms, which become the "hug."

Have an adult write, "I love you!" on the hugs, and have children decorate them with heart stickers and coloring.

After your children have completed the hugs, have them give themselves and one another "hugs from God." Suggest that the children make more hugs at home and send them to friends, relatives, and neighbors.

**ASK:**
- How do you think the prodigal son felt when his father hugged him?
- How did the father feel toward his lost son?
- How does God feel about you?
- Is there anything you could do that would make God's love for you disappear?

**BIBLE FOCUS:**

We are important
to God.

**BIBLE WORDS:**

" 'He was lost and is
found.' So they began to
celebrate" (Luke 15:24b).

**BIBLE STORY:**

# The Prodigal Son

**A** boy ran away from his father. The father was very worried
and never stopped loving his son. When the boy finally
returned, instead of being mad, the father rejoiced that his lost
son was now home. Use this craft to show kids how a missing boy
can appear on their papers. The children will enjoy making other
items appear and talking about how happy it makes them to see
things come back.

## THE LOST IS FOUND

**MATERIALS:**

For each child, you will
need the following:

- A cardboard cutout
  of a boy

- Crayons, preferably
  with no wrappers on
  them; one must be a
  dark color

- White, thin paper

- Optional: buttons;
  feathers; leaves; small,
  flat classroom objects

# How to make "The Lost Is Found"

Before children arrive, cut out from sturdy paper or cardboard outlines of a boy.

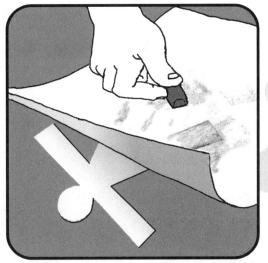

Have the children put boy cutouts under paper and use the wide sides of crayons to rub across their paper.

When they've finished their rubbings, have children add facial features with a dark crayon. On the papers, have an adult write, "Welcome Back."

Use rubbings of other objects, such as buttons, zippers, or bottoms of shoes, to add detail to the picture of the boy.

After you've told the story of the Prodigal Son, ask children if they can see on their paper the boy who ran away. The father was very sad and really wanted the boy to come home. Encourage children to help the boy come home by coloring with the edge of a crayon.

## ASK:
- How do you think the father felt when his son was lost?
- God is our Father. How do you think he would feel if we ran away from him?
- Can you tell me about a time when you lost something? How did you feel?
- What can you do if you feel sad about losing something?

**BIBLE FOCUS:**
Trust in Jesus.

**BIBLE WORDS:**
"It is I; don't be afraid"
(John 6:20b).

**BIBLE STORY:**
# Jesus Walks on Water

Jesus' disciples were in a boat when a strong wind made the water rough. Suddenly, they saw Jesus coming toward them; he was walking on water! He said, "It is I; don't be afraid." Use this clever project to act out the story of Jesus walking on water.

# WALKING ON WATER

**MATERIALS:**
For each child, you will need the following:

- Quart-sized resealable plastic freezer bags
- Copies of the picture of Jesus on page 95
- Crayons or markers
- Scissors
- Glue mixed with blue food coloring on a disposable pie plate
- Paintbrushes

# How to make "Walking on Water"

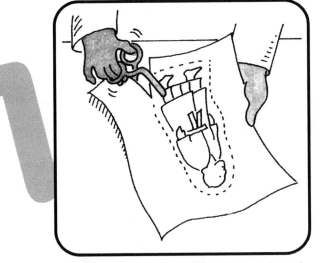

**Before children arrive, make copies of the picture on page 95. Have children color the picture of Jesus and cut it out.**

**Have children each put a picture in a plastic bag and seal the top.**

**Now, with the glue mixture, have kids paint waves under Jesus' feet.**

**After the glue dries, the children can peel it off and act out the story.**

After you have made your walking-on-water picture, discuss the following:

**ASK:**
- Who do you trust? Why?
- Why can you always trust Jesus?

## BIBLE PASSAGES:

*Matthew 14:22-33;*
*Mark 6:47-51;*
*John 6:16-21*

## BIBLE FOCUS:

Jesus is powerful.

## BIBLE WORDS:

"They saw Jesus...
walking on the water"
(John 6:19b).

# Jesus Walks on Water

**J**esus' disciples left him on the mountain to pray while they attempted to row to the other side of the lake. After praying, Jesus decided to join them, so he headed out on foot across the lake. Use this craft to help your little ones discover Jesus' power.

# MOVING ACROSS

## MATERIALS:

For each child, you will need the following:

- Small, plastic play figure
- Clean, empty butter tub with lid
- Two peel-and-stick magnet strips
- Unsharpened pencil
- Blue plastic wrap
- Rubber band

# How to make "Moving Across"

**Before children arrive, cut a small hole in the bottom center of each butter tub. Make the holes large enough for a pencil to fit through.**

**Have children each place peel-and-stick magnetic strips to the bottom of a plastic play figure and to the eraser of a pencil.**

**Now have children each slide the pencil through the hole in the bottom of the butter tub so that the magnet end of the pencil is inside the tub.**

**With rubber bands, help children secure the blue plastic wrap to the tops of their butter tubs (with the lids on).**

After children have completed their crafts, have them each place "Jesus" on the top of the "water" and use the magnet on the top of the pencil to make him walk. Have them act out the story of Jesus walking on water.

**ASK:**

- How do you think Jesus felt when the disciples were afraid of him?
- What would you have done if you were one of the disciples in the boat? Would you have wanted to walk on water as Peter did?
- What are some other ways that Jesus shows his power?

## BIBLE PASSAGES:
*Matthew 18:12-14;*
*Luke 15:3-7*

## BIBLE FOCUS:
God loves me.

## BIBLE WORDS:
"I have loved you with an everlasting love" (Jeremiah 31:3b).

## BIBLE STORY:
# The Lost Sheep

To help us understand God's love, Jesus told the story of a shepherd who set out in search of a sheep that had wandered away. When he found it, he placed it on his shoulders and carried it back to the safety of the fold. His neighbors and friends came out to rejoice with him over the return of the lost sheep. God, like the shepherd, seeks those who are lost, and when a sinful heart turns to him, heaven rejoices.

# HIDDEN SHEEP GAME

## MATERIALS:
For each child, you will need the following:

- Five identical plastic jar lids, large enough to place the sticker on
- Tempera paint
- Paintbrush
- One sticker of a sheep
- Paper to cover work surface

# How to make the "Hidden Sheep Game"

Prepare a work area where the children can paint.

Have children paint all the lids the same color.

When the paint has dried, have children each put a lamb sticker on the underside of one lid.

Have children ask a friend to guess under which lid the sheep is hiding.

No one can hide from God. No one can run from God. Our Shepherd, Jesus, cares for his sheep and will seek those who are lost. As the children play the Hidden Sheep Game, remind them of God's love for them.

**ASK:**
- How are we like sheep?
- How is Jesus like a shepherd?
- How does the shepherd feel about his sheep?

**BIBLE PASSAGES:**
*Matthew 18:12-14;*
*Luke 15:3-7*

**BIBLE FOCUS:**
God cares for me.

**BIBLE WORDS:**
"Rejoice with me; I have found my lost sheep" (Luke 15:6b).

## BIBLE STORY:
# The Lost Sheep

Ashepherd was taking care of his sheep. He kept a watchful eye over them and noticed that one sheep was missing. The shepherd thought all of the sheep were very special. He would keep looking until he found the lost sheep. Use this craft to help your little ones experience the story of the missing sheep and find out that they, too, are special in God's eyes.

# SPECIAL SHEEP

**MATERIALS:**
For each child, you will need the following:

● Cotton balls

● Glue

● One craft stick with the words "_____ is special" written on it

● Green Easter grass, or have kids cut small pieces of green paper

● A sheep outline cut out of sturdy paper

# How to make "Special Sheep"

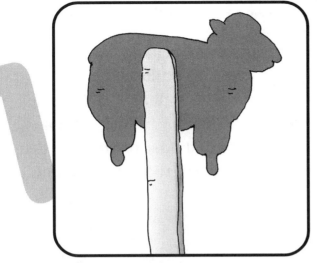

**Before children arrive, make enough sheep on sturdy paper for everyone. Glue a craft stick to each sheep, and let it dry before children arrive.**

**Have children glue cotton to the side of the sheep with the faces.**

**Have kids glue Easter grass or cut-up green paper pieces to the other side.**

**On the sticks before the words "is special," help children write their names.**

After they have completed their sheep, have kids hold them up. Have only one child hold his or her sheep so that the grass side is showing. Say, "Oh, no! One of my sheep is missing. I must go find it. It is special to me." Have children look around to see who has the grass side out. When they've found the sheep, have kids take turns hiding their sheep. Continue playing until everyone has a turn to hide his or her sheep.

## ASK:
- How do you think the shepherd felt as he looked for his sheep?
- Have you ever lost something important to you and then found it?
- How can you show someone they are very special to you?

**BIBLE PASSAGES:**
*Matthew 27:22–28;*
*Mark 15–16:8;*
*Luke 23:33–24:12;*
*John 19–20:18*

**BIBLE FOCUS:**
Jesus died for me.

**BIBLE WORDS:**
"Christ died for our sins"
(1 Corinthians 15:3b).

## BIBLE STORY:

# Jesus' Death and Resurrection

**C**hrist's death on the cross paid the penalty for sin and opened the way of forgiveness. As children learn of Christ's death and resurrection, they can begin to understand the concept of sin and their need for a Savior. The cross is the symbol of God's provision for mankind and a visual reminder of the fact that the chains of sin have been broken and eternal life is available to any who will receive it by faith.

# PUZZLE-PIECE CROSS

**MATERIALS:**

For each child, you will need the following:

● One 6½-inch cardboard cross

● Small jigsaw puzzle pieces

● Glue

● 6-inch piece of yarn or string

**90** I Can Make It Myself!

# How to make the "Puzzle-Piece Cross"

**1**

Ahead of time, cut one cardboard cross for each child and punch a hole in the top.

**2**

Have children cover the cross by gluing on puzzle pieces.

**3**

Have kids glue on another layer of overlapping puzzle pieces.

**4**

When the glue has dried, tie a piece of yarn through the top of each cross.

Like placing the puzzle pieces on the cross, our sin was placed on Christ. He paid the price of sin and offered the gift of salvation to all. To help children personalize these concepts,

**ASK:**
● For whom did Christ die?
● What did Christ's death provide?
● How can you be forgiven?

## BIBLE PASSAGES:
*Matthew 27:22–28;*
*Mark 15–16:8;*
*Luke 23:33–24:12;*
*John 19–20:18*

## BIBLE FOCUS:
Jesus lives!

## BIBLE WORDS:
"He has risen!"
(Mark 16:6b).

## BIBLE STORY:
# Jesus' Death and Resurrection

**T**hree days after his crucifixion, Jesus' followers discovered that his tomb was empty. Although the Gospels vary in how they explain the disciples' discovery of this event, all tell the good news of Jesus' power over death. Use this craft to help children imagine the wonder of that first Easter morning and then share the good news of Jesus' resurrection with others.

RESURRECTION T-SHIRTS

## MATERIALS:
For each child, you will need the following:
- White cotton T-shirt
- Red, orange, and yellow fabric paint
- Painting sponges
- Self-adhesive paper (Contact paper)
- Newspaper

**92**    I Can Make It Myself!

# How to make the "Resurrection T-Shirts"

Before children arrive, place folded newspaper inside each T-shirt.

Help each child stick the self-adhesive paper to the shirt in a figure of the risen Christ. Have them sponge paint on and around the figures to create a sunrise effect.

Have an adult peel the self-adhesive paper from the T-shirt while the paint is still damp.

When the paint has dried completely, have an adult remove the newspaper and launder the shirt according to the manufacturer's directions, printed on the paint containers.

After the children have completed their T-shirts, read the story of the resurrection to them.

## ASK:
- Why was Jesus' tomb empty?
- How does the story of Jesus' resurrection make you feel?
- How can you share this good news with others?

Group Publishing, Inc.
Attention: Product Development
P.O. Box 481
Loveland, CO 80539
Fax: (970) 679-4370

**Evaluation for**
*I Can Make It Myself!*

Please help Group Publishing, Inc. continue to provide innovative and useful resources for ministry. Please take a moment to fill out this evaluation and mail or fax it to us. Thanks!

● ● ●

1. As a whole, this book has been (circle one)

not very helpful                                            very helpful

1      2      3      4      5      6      7      8      9      10

2. The best things about this book:



3. Ways this book could be improved:



4. Things I will change because of this book:



5. Other books I'd like to see Group publish in the future:



6. Would you be interested in field-testing future Group products and giving us your feedback? If so, please fill in the information below:

Name _____

Church Name _____

Denomination _____ Church Size _____

Church Address _____

City _____ State _____ ZIP _____

Church Phone _____

E-mail _____